INVICTUS

INVICTUS

poems

of late and earlier

RODNEY NELSON

2019

INVICTUS: Poems of Late and Earlier
Copyright © 2019 Rodney Nelson
All rights reserved.

ISBN 978-1-7335979-0-6

Published by Middle Island Press
PO Box 354
West Union WV 26456

Contents

Acknowledgments — xi

Poems — 1

2018 — 3

COME THE OTHER	5
OF NOW	6
BROWN STUDY	7
MAYBE TO SERVE	8
OLD MAN IN OCTOBER	9
THEIR DESERTS	10
INVICTUS	11
UNKNOWABLE	12
THE RUN	13
HOLING UP	14
LOOK AT THAT PILE	15
EARLY AFTERNOON	16
A PLACE	17
TWELVE TWENTY-FIVE SEVENTEEN	18
THE COLD	19
NORWEGIAN EYE	20
I AM HERE	21
SOME DIFFERENT ENDING	22
A MAMMAL'S PLACE	23
TONIGHT	24
MIDMORNING SUN	25
THE VAST OF IT	26
KAWABATA WAKING	27
LOOKING FOR SPRING	28
BEACH COMBER	29
GONE AMISS	30
DISTENDED WINTER	31

A DIG	32
PREFATORIES	33
DAY'S END	34
RELEASED	35
BUMPING INTO MAY	36
RIVERSIDE	37
PUB	38
TO SOMEONE I WANT TO MEET	39
NOT TALKING	40
OTHER ONES	41
FARMER TRACTS	42
BUTTES IN JUNE	43
RES PUBLICA	44
CHILD IN THE EPIDEMIC	45
ROBIN	46
UNDER GROVE	47
WEALTH	48
WILL'S RETRUN	49
LOVE	50
ANTONY OLDKNOW IN DREAM ACTION	51
THE PLAN	52
DIRIGO	53
THE SOUND OF MOTION	54
IN THE GALLERY WOODS	55
CLOSING UP	56
ONLY TWO	57
STOR PER JANSSON	58
FORSTER NOW	59
2012	61
PARKS IN JUNE	63
THISTLE	64
PLAINS HEAT	65
IN WAIT	66
AN INTERRUPTION	67

AN ONLY ONE	68
HEARTHSTONE	69
NINE-ONE	70
AFTER A DEATH	71
SEPTEMBER FULLING	72
WE FIVE	73
WHAT IS AND WILL COME	74
TRIP NOTES	75
WEATHER WIND	76
BUTTE	77
WIDENING THE ZONE	78
DAUGHTER	79
VACANT FARMSTEAD IN AUTUMN	80
CHICKEN WIRE	82
LIVE TO TELL	84
NOVEMBER MORNING	85
GO TO THE CAW	86
LINES TO A POTTER	88
VACANT FARMSTEAD IN WINTER	89
MEDLEYS	90
A YEAR AND TWO DEATHS	91
MAKING IT BOON	92
CONSIDERING	93
WINTER CHRONICLE	94
TAKEN EAST	95
2010	**97**
YOUNG IN THE CITY	99
EXOTERICA	100
AIRPORT IN AUGUST	101
FOR TWO	102
SKILLMAN LANE	103
CITY NIGHTS	105
DAY FALL	106
ACCORD IN MENDOCINO	107

PARTS IN YOUR LIFE	108
QUISCALES DE MÉJICO	109
IF WE WERE	110
SONOMA	111
EDUCATION	112
THE WINE OF IT	113
IT SEEMED	114
TRUTH IN SAN FRANCISCO	115
OREGONIAN TEXT	116
NO RETURN	117
ARISE	118
2008	119
CAMP ON THE LITTLE MISSOURI	121
JULY IN WYOMING	122
REST STOP	123
EAST OF WALLA WALLA	124
SUMMER RANGE	125
DRIFTER'S TUNE	126
BADLANDS OF A METACOWBOY	127
BELONG	128
METACOWBOY LETS ON TO CATTLE KATE	129
CHANSON DE GESTE OF A METACOWBOY	130
SCION OF A COPPERHEAD	131
CHANTS FROM "NO ONE OTHER"	132
OUT	135
NOTE TO MIAMI BEACH	137
YELLOW SPRINGS	138
POET GUY IN AMERICA	139
OUT OF SEDONA	140
METACOWBOY	141
CANYON	142
OLD SONG	143
ANY HOUR	144
EVEN THE WORD	146

NOTA BENE	147
FROM SCRATCH	148
BREAK OF MARCH	150
YUMA HAT	151
ANY OTHER	153
JOHN WAHL	154
METACOWBOY AT APRIL'S END	155
POWDER RIVER	156
Biography	157

ACKNOWLEDGMENTS

63 Channels, Arts Forum, Big Bridge, Cowboy Poetry Press, Hamilton Stone Review, High Plains Register, Literateur, Milk and Honey, Nostrovia, Open, People's Press Project, Plainsongs Poetry Magazine, Poetry Bay, Prairie Wolf Press Review, Remington Review, Retort, Sandstar Review, Sierra Journal, Straitjackets, and *Unlikely Stories*

The 2012 section originally appeared as the chapbook *In Wait* under the imprint of Night Bomb Press in that year.

The 2008 section originally appeared as the chapbook *Metacowboy* under the imprint of The Moon Publishing & Printing in 2011. "Chants from 'No One Other'" had appeared in *Big Bridge* as parts of the narrative poem "No One Other."

Poems

2018

COME THE OTHER

the year had an out side too
and that was where you met it
at the turning in late spring
and with all the light and heat
over lake-land and prairie
you did not travel sun-shy
so that you would be ready
for early night and retreat
to chair and studio lamp
come the in side of the year

OF NOW

you had to ride a ways to catch the mottling
of tree leaves and many other

                      to the eye
their evidence was incontrovertible
in town as well but the day needed quiet
so you had to find an outpost grove at the
prairie's rim and a sunny log as back-prop
if you wanted a line of insight into
the motley that time was up to arranging
         while it blanched you
like bone or snag you might have
reflected as a flappable old human
yet knew that you too would be lying white in
the crabgrass of next April or towering
without color into its sky and the leaves
of now would have gone nondiscrete on damp ground

                    the birds
of now were here and did not see you

BROWN STUDY

before the day of squirrel and me
there must have been a flicking move in
the undergrowth that needed squirrel
to take on a body and make it
    and at that time
there would have come wind
to buckle the tallgrass like the one
I am hearing now in man-sown corn
        am listening for
a catch to it
    a change to howl
that will run me off
and the muted cluck of river on
its turn to roar in that early day
would have had not anyone to scare
        no me or other
like the squirrel
I am watching as I think about
its coloration and the acorn's
and wood of oak
    awaiting fire

MAYBE TO SERVE

every thought of mine is stray and
I cannot assume the maple tree
in peach-rose leaf I met on a walk
by the river will define my day
when I gather its all in writing
    no I have
to remember one thought
about politics and another
on my sink toward the cold of age
with autumn and many more that are
eluding me now
        but maybe I
ignore what every peach-rose leaf
of the tree is here to have me think
    maybe I have taken the walk and
met the maple only to serve it

OLD MAN IN OCTOBER

step out into the large
and heaving day
    get weak
inside your rib cage
        squint
and know it to be fall

there is too much around
for you to take
    more wind
than a man can face
      so
you want to go back in

sway forth and let the day
bulge over you
    inhale
its cracked-wood doings
      bow
to a flare of shading

THEIR DESERTS

a hard too-early winter wind
came on at their reward picnic
but they did not leave
        kept chewing
for they had earned this cold chicken
and the park was tolerable
in many other ways or it
had been
     and they had sat right here
in July and watched their daughters
sweat at tennis while the odor
of pool chlorine imbued the heat
        leaving room
for the sweeter reek
of heartwood from a blown-down tree
so having known ease in the park
they would not give way to this wind
     would eat
their deserts to the bone
until the return of glory

INVICTUS

I am the relict of a tribe that did
not number many
        have survived among
the alien as an anonym of
so meager windage they mistake it for
debility

    I would not recognize
my fellow others if I saw them if
any there be
        such numbered few we were
in the old open but our homeland
is the planet

    and so it will remain
no matter how the alien many
take and bleach it
        burn and cover the earth
we walked as earth to mountains we could see
until the rising vapor grayed them out

UNKNOWABLE

they had a name for what they saw
on the powdery township road
and knew a genealogy
to fit the boy into
     yet he
was none of them nor would he be
the young man in a tie and coat
they might have looked at as he ran
toward an office building on
the hillside of a port city
              no he
would not be that nor was
the hale white-whiskered one the friend
that other hikers took him for
along a mountain's stony trail
above the high desert

     what seemed
to them like a winnowed codger
at a bird refuge ten miles into
the prairie bog was neither man
nor any knowable creature
           only
a cryptid in disguise
a cryptid seeking out a hole
to hide his every bone in

THE RUN

the ones that grew you put you wayward
on a mountain road in the day's shank
on a highway bent along the coast
on the great and flat and achy route from
the Bois de Sioux to Río Bravo
and there was city too
    but their lent
momentum did not let
you stop so you would arrive nowhere
and have to travel years beyond it
until age wound you down
             made you pull
into the shade of cliff or garden
of even a silo on the plain
and know at last you wouldn't have had
to run wayward to reach this quiet

HOLING UP

the olden time of the northern peasant
went on millennia and even now
there is an urge to cavern in late fall
    seek the hearth
to mend the nets and whittle
and read from pattern or book
           even with
electric means to keep the night and chill
off-limited and a way for talking
to inmates of another dark elsewhere

and now there are south windows in the wall
to gather at on a midday of sun
    see the light out there
be weak but alive
and not a pining mere recollection

LOOK AT THAT PILE

if I had to be a child again
I would live in the woods upriver
with a crippled dad and I would take
and hoard scrap lumber from the site of
a onetime landing
     not thinking why
until a wind knocked down our hut
but let the two of us survive and
I could tell him to look at that pile
          we can rebuild
and then walk off to
the mudded bank and watch for turtle

EARLY AFTERNOON

the look of the day on prairie in a winter
of no snow brings an unremastered film to mind
    the sunlight jittery
with violins straining
not to go flat
                  the dialog creaking apart
but to leave the window and walk out into a
same weak light is to forget the recorded sound
    meet real day
and love the brown where the green was loved

A PLACE

I am at a concourse of grove and open
and the reach of sunup to a snag's dry wood
has given me a minute of overjoy
    which I'd feel too
if I were prehuman with
only an eye a nose an ear a tongue and
a paw to let me hunt out the music here
        no memory
of whatever was that went
that left me not to mourn but wanting the rise
of dawn in motile air to happen again
and I have a name and the hang of naming
    have waited
in open and grove where no one
of my kind has been
        marked this patch at the foot
of some other millennium for return
    where the minute is enclaved
time upon time
but I can't put it into a phrase or tune

TWELVE TWENTY-FIVE SEVENTEEN

the day in clarity and cold has
no lowering to it
    only sun
without dominion and quiet
without a break
    and you cannot damn
the place or the time where you hunker
and huddle
    rabbitlike in the snow
nor deject you on settling for this
    when you might
have been rampant today
in gloriation of the same sun
along an antipodean beach

    you wanted
your wanting country of
origin to arrange your bones in
and the cards agreed
    winter or not

THE COLD

at the edge of our business day and
our family night the animals wreak
a living on one another in the cold
          and some die now
some have to wait for the hook
of owl or the click of ermine or a thwack
up the roadway
     where some of us die with them
some have to wait until a gun comes out or
the radiation fails in the middle of
our business day
         and family night
and next to the animals and above them
a tree is cold-transfixed on a page of sky
we may want to read
     when we cross the margin

NORWEGIAN EYE

    what we beheld
           the grandfather and I
a wiry thicket where one rabbit's sign
went in on winter white
    might have been part
           of a Norwegian walk
that he had done
some early afternoon
   and next to him
          in my own boy time
I might have seen as
a party to his act of beholding
the track the way he did
    or through his mind
here on my home American prairie
looking up now at the same point of north
         he had known
    but from another angle

I AM HERE

Damastner Glanz des Schnees.
Darauf liest sich die Spur
Des Hasen, Finken, Rehs,
Der Wesen Signatur.

WILHELM LEHMANN

the look of the woods would have drawn a hunter
but only for what he had to do
    read what
a turkey or deer had printed on the snow
which he could follow to more of the message
replying to it with a shot

        I am here
for the winter look and the quiet only
with nothing to do yet I would have put on
any animal or human body just
to come to the woods and be
    read a print once

SOME DIFFERENT ENDING

every road of mine would end I thought
by the sea at a grandmother's cottage
or over it on the deck of a friend
and I would welcome every mile there
as though each one had been a saltier
    a more green
but now that most of my rides
like Grandmother and friends the like of him
are done I tend to wish I had waited
and taken the dry turn up the mountain
to give my part of noon to its summit
                easy and high
and in the quiet seen
the combers down ahead and back of me
the valley my right trip had started from

I would have met a porcupine maybe
and stayed a time and even claimed that road
as one of mine
    would even be there now

A MAMMAL'S PLACE

the snow and rain go down and I
do not want to be under that
    would rather go up
and one day
of unmitigated sunlight
at a bald cliff I have in me
a hanker to fly to the like
on the moon or Mars
        knowing I
can wright the means to make it there
and a shelter for my breathing

but not a way to stay too long
or of guarantying return
    because I am
a mammal of
the wet and warm and down here of
a wintry night when the cosmos
alights on my prairie I've got
a retreat at hand
        a walled nest
that quiet frigid space cannot
infuse while I'm the maintainer

TONIGHT

you are clamped to rooms in late winter
only if you mean to carry through
    to wait on relief
and you don't need
to pin your night's view to the carpet
where the shadow from a lamplight is
made weakly by one from another
       no you
can look out there and go too
into the resident cold and dark
now that you have no one left to say
a *goodbye* to
    take care
        we'll see you
because the wording did not weigh much
even then
    just the pain and regret
of the sayer and who watched and heard
so you can leave without talk tonight
without mourning as Orion must
have been intent to do
     take the way
from winter toward his part of sky

MIDMORNING SUN

the oaken table on the deck
is not for platters anymore

every scrap of thought of food
was trayed and trundled in with night

let one tipped chair be evidence
of all the talk that rang out here

now at the swelling light is time
to lay a book on the table

take up the new hard clarity
each word of few is burning with

and let whatever it may mean
be signal in midafternoon

THE VAST OF IT

I might not have gone to such an overlook if
some other had not made me retreat to it or
yet another guided me there so in my mind
I tied the place to whoever had been and let
the mountain and the view of forest and vineyard
belong to one or both
    the exhilaration
    of my being there too

with time and retreating into a solitude
I went to guide myself up the warm dusty trail
    find at the overlook
    that the setting and not
the others had mattered who had served only to
exile or walk me there so now I could breathe in
the vast of it and take a place on the Mount Saint
Helena of my own

KAWABATA WAKING

early March weather
each day an object lesson
who knows what it is

LOOKING FOR SPRING

the rooms have narrowed too much
to keep you in
    are nearing
accordance with the days' growth
on a field
       no birds of which
are here yet

    the blatant white
may seem disaccordant to
birds of which
      a worriment
but only the tightened rooms
spook you
    looking out from them

BEACHCOMBER

he did not go hunting float or shell at the sea
or only to look again on the peace of it
and nighttime heave

he had been rummy inland for the want of what
he could not say but felt on now returning to
headland and shore

even a cranky leg did not delay him and
the seal that widened an eye at the river's mouth
had been waiting

the makeup of the beach made him up too he could
not say but knew as he went footing on his own
home sand and wrack

GONE AMISS

they were afoot
    two men two women
and it should have been at a crossroad
out of town they had to stop
      but they
would not have needed to on their range
of lake and woody drumlin
    had gone
amiss and were not at home
      so it
had to be at an intersection
of twitchy light they waited around
and looked with nothing to do but live
    nowhere to do it in
then one of
the men began to orate in a
crackpot voice
        on and on and louder
until he talked up a direction
    went bungling into the crosswalk and
let the others grin and traipse after

DISTENDED WINTER

the higher light of April cued me
to wake up again but spring did not
occur to the prairie so I had
a list of only expectations
in my head
      the turf's return to green
an arriving robin's bob and run
the ice-out on the river
            but I
wanted more than memory to write
them down from and would have had to do
a squinty walk in the naked woods
and the open and catch a real whiff
      to get the wording
for this one time

A DIG

not in the charnel of a buried city
would they find it
    no the white fragment of a
human tibia would provoke their dig in
an arroyo up a mountain of few trees
and enduring light and heat
       swigging water
they would unearth and mark and lay out the rest

would see it might have tumbled here
    rock to rock
but I not they am who to say that it might
have wanted this on the downclimb from a height
of bristlecone
       not that I could have chosen
to remain it
    no I had left the bone-strew
and meant it only to tell them I had been

PREFATORIES

the mild arrived in private
after my wintry wait
but the river woods showed it
in a humbler than green
at the side of the fringe trail
under strident daylight
and with not a leaf or wind
or bird to educe me
the tune I would have joined in
remained an idea

DAY'S END

FOR AEM

    we two made camp
           a waypoint for
      overnight in
northwest pineland
and doing the work she smiled though
not at me

           a gray jay was on
the table and went
      was again
but her smile meant to include the
stretch we had ridden
           the long road

I had set us to
      her liking
of all of it now we had reached
a patch in what we were out for
           could cede
the day's end to a bird

her smiling humbled me
      showed me
as only a part of the where
we went and how
           and many jays
would be and go and be again

RELEASED

    warm hard south wind
        a walloping
    in the unleaved grove
            a tousler
    of dry brown weed and undergrowth
    and a cottonwood winnower
        sprung wind
    for the migratories
    to flow up on
           for northerners
    to bolt the dugout
        and bathe in

BUMPING INTO MAY

and every other catkin might
not have come down had there been no rain
to sluice the tree
     and why do I take
a first granting of dandelion
as a reminder or prompt
               a sign
when even in my decay I would
not know of what
     looking with caution
at a river of indiscipline
             hearing
the birds' mate-calls around it

RIVERSIDE

on the bank the cottonwood's spread out not up
to make a bowering for the vagrant in
a day of heat
    a shading at the river
and the quick new greens along the pathway did
enliven me

      I am thankful to return
and would sing of it if I knew that a tune
was welcome now
    would parade among my kind
in cap and bells and tattoo if I wanted
to go down singing

      they do not merit song
however and would have to see through my act
in a time of no public joy
    so I'll keep
to me what I might have warbled about on
the green path and in the riverside bower

PUB

there is baby talk in
one of the booths and I
remember a cartoon
    a magazine

it is an afternoon
of antipoetry
in a cartoon of room
    a magazine

TO SOMEONE I WANT TO MEET

I would ask you to go or come with me
to a certain park at a time like now
and watch the wind
     northern and big
            not cold
when it takes on the new viridity
of the leaves it has become aloud in
     and I mean both
a look and a green sound
          would ask you to
because none that I know
would want to go or come in the park now
and heed a wind
     or me as I show you
a certain tree that has been putting out
too few leaves each spring
          and will turn to snag
     dumb in wind
until the same or fire
renders it down
          and at the riverbank
we'll see how floods have half-unrooted it

NOT TALKING

if I squint my thinking long enough
I can make out a day of valleys
that are not perceptible to me
    or have not been
a day or venue
the ruck have not yet gotten into
and of burgeoning hills I would live
to visit if I had more shadow
to offer in May
          but calling it
one place in time or out would fire
the others to cry Eden and there
is not only one of anywhere
    or has not been
so I'm not talking

OTHER ONES

my quiet and the solitude
have pooled to let me go and be
some other in another time
and now I'm at the window of
a country church
      no one around
the smell of yard grass drifting in
on a morning in June I think
but can't tell who or what has done
the mowing so open the door
          look out
and there is a goatherd
with animals at work and when
he nods at me I have to be
some other in another time
     in the
café I make out now
where I can sit at a table
so long as I remain alone
and do not talk and no one turns
to look or nod
           but why should I
go on with it when all I want
is to hear my name from someone

FARMER TRACTS

go east overland to where they abide
in the calm of fields but on city time
now turn to the trees
    higher and darker
more heavy-leaved than any name for them
                  the groves'
impenetrability
a look that moving in wind enhances
to bring out the lineaments
    of here

BUTTES IN JUNE

indignities have been the few
among the unarrested pine
    the none on high
white rock where men
might have gone up to sentinel
if they'd had cause to muster here
or even camp

        a battle and
uranium drew few again
only to pass but not as would
and will the dignitaries crow
and hawk
    are doing now all day

RES PUBLICA 2018

the wise and hardy common man
of democratic yarn turned out
to be a solipsist and now
you're told and even shown it
on the phone and in a year like this
of microcephaly you do
not want to flaunt your normal head
when the others parade

     there is
a road to take away and to
and you know where the quiet zone
begins so you may sputter in
a bucket once the horns and flags
that came at you are over but
do not omit to laugh and laugh
as you get out of here to there

CHILD IN THE EPIDEMIC

midsummer day you have awaited
    the borders of it
    remote from noon
and now are walking a wagon trail
on a black rut
        weeds in bloom along
        either side
but light and heat and scent
too heavy for you to move under
    the windlessness
    not any relief
and the weight to let you get only
to the badger patch they have warned of
        where an unseen crippler
        will jump out

ROBIN

and robins add only a sight to
the fear and boredom of a village
    take only worms away
as a half-
attentive watcher at the window
would agree
        seeing them at work on
a cloudy green forenoon then turning
to the notebook page
    yet in that sight
is the name robin with all of its
inhering color
        its movement and
unforgotten call so there will be
a double adding to the village
    when watcher puts *robin*
on paper

UNDER GROVE

all any day the trees are there
and move only on the wind's own
or fire's some rare time but down
at root a pulse goes out
                    comes in
one tree from another or to
that legg'd creatures of open air
can't sense

    let one tree feel the axe
or have a break during storm and
the others know
                fungi having
relayed the pulse in code to each
so now they're making ready to
maintain the grove and further it
    to seal and heal all any night

WEALTH

the grandparents would be in town all day, entrusting the farm to him, a boy of twelve, and as he watched the old coupe go smaller he felt a privacy surround him that he could not own but did, the riches of grove and yard becoming his now, so if people drove up he would eye them from a hedge of chokecherry, not show, keep day and place to himself, maybe tell the grandparents later, and even in age I like to be alone with harboring nature, every leaf scent meant for me, but if the coupe did not return toward evening I would panic, drive to the next farm, to another, no one around at either, no lights coming on, say to myself they've abandoned me I'm dying, whereas the boy of twelve would have trusted a world he did not know, sensing that all the food and drink in the country would be his if other people were gone, waited meanwhile in his wealth of time

WILL'S RETURN

if he were at the words again he'd be
a tragicomic on the human and
no longer hidden in his love but would
not find a stage to take the drama to
so have to write for screen or even page

nonviewing recluse that I am I'd catch
him on the latter in the tone of what
he's written now about the rain and its
untame arriving scent throughout the wold
and under any byline I'd hear him

LOVE

they took a picnic table under a high rustling cottonwood in the riverside park, man and woman of fifty or so, thick and plain yet animated, arching forward, ready to smile, which might have meant they had not been a couple until now or for decades but anyway had found each other and agreed to share the perfection of July out here, futurity in mind maybe, beer and crackers on the tabletop, and who knew how either one together or apart would look back on this trial outing, from marriage and its sure warmth or with the eye of a bitter aging isolate or in grief over what had not yet befallen when they sat and talked and watched a duck or two on the far bank, each trying to pick words that would ease the other and not add to the impersonality of the tree's sound in wind above them

ANTONY OLDKNOW IN DREAM ACTION

a half-mile run before dinner
he would have gone on anywhere
and anytime
    even the night
of the banquet which reminded
the other faculty they had
a redcoat in their midst
            not just
one more poet but Antony
jogged out in faith and honest lack
of cockiness though had he met
a game hen
    heading or waiting
he might have broken rhythm and
made cause with her
            chitchatted up
an episode of scarves and what-
ever the outcome have circled
back to the hall
    poured a sherry
and ignored the looks that meant to
immure the night
          the fall
    and him

THE PLAN

when I abandon rooms
for good I'll want to be
alive and moving on
my own so that I don't
forget to take the ax
I left out there somehow
to weather even though
the head of it is gone

I may remember too
its sound on black walnut
even the heartwood's scent
but more I'll want to hear
a fanfare in the grove
and see the bright of it
marking my old time's end
to trumpet in a new

DIRIGO

     and water is
the medium for reversion
so to be viewed from shore
                          drunk or laved in
    blessed with
and in the desert guided
                          but not swum in or
embarked upon as if to seek return to an
impossible age of origin
    no your grant
is land and you must march high and away to keep
the dry the medium of advance
                       configure
with dirt and rock and ash and bone while rain and flood
come only to go
     though you may turn and look down
at sunlight's movement on bay
                        never regretting

THE SOUND OF MOTION

of the valley or the end of summer's full
I could have said it waited or that it was
at a standstill though not the kind of motion
the place or the time had been in or what had
brought it to this
                but of the quiet and hues
the wind had left I did say rich and hearing
one dove times one give a call not a reply
I readied for scant-moon night midway in which
were one coyote times three
      yips of motion

IN THE GALLERY WOODS

in prehistory early on I would bide
to watch the birds as I do now but only
the ones to take
     only to tell the hunters
where to find them and the young men would heed me
in that I knew and could see what they did not

the tribe would have been tending to and feeding
this remnant of me by then who had become
a one to leave
     behind in June or outside
in January yet while my old eye saw
I could bide and dawdle as I do today

CLOSING UP

small birds that had animated the grove
in June were not around for the ending
of August
    but more seemed to be missing
the quiet too large
        so I tried to name
each thing I ought to have heard or seen here
in the welcoming fulsome greens

    I could
not think of any and maybe it was
repletion not an absence I took in
        a time coming perfect
to its still end
having done so uncounted times before
in grove and open alike
    the aim of
it all to be a routine closing up
        a move on
without equivocation

ONLY TWO

if I wanted to forestall
the sweetening of apple
    the asters' bloom
I would do
an accounting or counting
of the ways to waylay time
    would find
there are two choices
    to go analphabetic
    at the woods' taking color
or go out altogether

STOR PER JANSSON

the big man from old iron hills
mined soft earth here and his swing plow
could furrow on to the point where
the sun downed and a dream began
of generations he would seed
throughout a prairie named for him

work sweated up the big man who
could see the myriad of farms
and grandchildren already not
the loss of all to time and change
the flight to wait and die in town
away from the smell of plowing

nor would he've whoa'd the team to think
about an owl in the old land
and how its hunt went on and on
or one in woods of river here
that would not turn but watched the last
new van get packed and trundle off

FORSTER NOW

time to get you out

why be myrmidon
with a dumb phone grin
in the gossip show

when you can meet trees
of reality
on earth you have walked

only disconnect

2012

PARKS IN JUNE

ONE

where the path got out of oak shade
onto an open ridge I thought
about the cardinal and what
its red meant to say to the eye
of bird or other animal
including me and would the song
convey it too
                I did not see
any cardinal that day and
someone I knew too well would not
even have wanted to come up
on the ridge to look and think

TWO

the woods of a more pointed green
were waiting heavy for the wind
to return and I could have walked
the wet they stood in but I had
a lookout tower to try me
     I overtopped the trees somewhere
about eighty feet and at a
hundred twenty I caught the view
              how far
onto the giant lake
and off to hillocks in country
I would never visit I had
hoped to see who knew and someone
I knew too well was tired of
the earth and would not have wanted
to climb and look on its reach

THISTLE

on the first or last or other day
of anyone a north wind parted
the heat keeping the mosquitoes low
   tumbleweed were tall
and out in front
and bloom to make a declaration
along the prairie road
    I took in
their scent and violet and tried to
imagine how a leaf or a root
would do on my tongue
   what the other
in our wry union of two
against the family and mankind
     now as in childhood
would think and have
to add to our understanding
that men and women often were wrong
   a plant never at all
not even
a root-loose intruder on the first
or last or other day
    I tried to
imagine how I would do as the
anyone left in the union
with a sister gone
   with only the
declared livingness of tumbleweed

PLAINS HEAT

the air had a trammel on or in it
so an animal got heavy trying
to move into shade
        worked at waiting there
and a wash more gray than blue overhead
invited no one out to the open
beyond a stand of trees that did not have
a name anymore
        the tiny birds used
to have one and would in Calcutta but
not around the town of Hannaford
        news
that a tornado had hit near to it
relieved an animal's mind in the wet
and hampered grove
            something had moved at least

IN WAIT

a brown house in the green farm country
and summer heat to make it all one

a dragonfly on a lightning rod
up on the ridge of the roof to wait

a woman in the window seeing
the garden pull away into weed

a nuthatch at the empty feeder
to check it one more time and again

a woman dying in the window
with an eye on garden and driveway

to make it all one and summer heat
and a tired house in farm country

but a dragonfly up on the ridge
of the roof and gone and returning

a dragonfly on a lightning rod
in wait and watch at the treetops' height

AN INTERRUPTION

and birth took her out of the sleep
into the waking garden where
she contented to be and play
until they came talking for her

but there were hedges of childhood
that maintained quiet in hiding
where bird and mammal and the green
had little to say or nothing

when time gave her a womanhood
to the extent of the garden
and they came on to talk and look
she turned to the wine for haven

and did not have to hear even
bird and mammal or see the green
as all waking ended there and
the wine returned her to the sleep

AN ONLY ONE

BLNK

I think of the dead
       not one
a many and not an each

but a they did not wait in
a window
       watch the garden
a they had left untended
or resign over time to
becoming the rain field and
its catchment

       only a one
could have read what the weather
seemed to write
       taken it bad

there are no dead I think and
one that went is only not

HEARTHSTONE

yes I have been the venturing one
on sea and in archipelago
and where the red rocks come to mountain
but I never got the beauty of
a north-woods lake until I wrote them
at home of it
      the relief of the
open it gave the forest trekker
made the lake so and who were reading
at the hearth completed my notion

yes I have mailed or taken the news
to the only at home and later
the one but now the hearth is quiet
with nobody to help me get the
meaning of a river and I may
not venture again
      but if I do
I may go on until I am a
bone sack where every trail is meant
to end and find the old hearthstone there

NINE-ONE

all it needed was a fit or two of rain
to make a shadow at midday and people
were going away in important cars from
the misdeed of summer that had been their own
                          maybe the heat
would hurry out after them
and buildings assume a wanted role again
but the sun came through and vegetation in
the graveyard went on rotting and the trees knelt
into another month of tumid river
                        the pavement
had an odor of misdoing

AFTER A DEATH

I want the old things now
      a wooden cigar box
         a type eraser and
      a gray-and-white photo
because the old are gone
and cannot tell me what
everything had meant
to the hands of them and
one of the few that knew
is not here anymore
to remember with me

I want the older things
      a bone-handled razor
         a checkered bowtie and
      a mug made in Sweden
because the touch of them
can tell what they had meant
and they have an odor
of going down in earth
because they are here now
along with the ashtray
of one that used to know

SEPTEMBER FULLING

the lake was day between the trees out there
with a boat and no wind to ripple it
and the evening came to a matter
of windlessness too and the lake to moon

the heavy dewing after sundown and
the insect hum from everywhere marked
an end to one more light time for the trees
that were as heavy in leaves and quiet

it came to one more hum before sunup
with crow racket and no other birds' and
where two brown leaves dropped to the summer ground
a yellowjacket fed on dragonfly

WE FIVE

the winter was not deep on the coast
we drove to talking a month beyond
its height
        the Brie and rolls and Rhine wine
had a taste of sun and a light of
the mild sea air to them
              we were in
the early time of our debauch
yet even the breath I'm drawing now
so late in my own has sea to it
        that one
              that sun too we took to eat
and drink of at a high winter's end
with a drift log for backrest
        talking

WHAT IS AND WILL COME

and the high unbroken hang of cloud
with no wind pressing it at the turn
to fall means every northerner
belongs to a tribe of the alone

and noontime sun on the next day or
the same could not be gentler with no
retreating green in blade or leaf
or hurry to bag up the acorns

but wind will return with enough snow
to make a whiteout of the rumpus
and drive every northern mind in
the hole for many nights' duration

but there will come a diminution
of even midwinter with color
to be seen on the gray oak bark and
an omen in the pearlier sky

TRIP NOTES

BADLAND

one insect and another but few more
in arcing flight above the horizon
of dry tall grass
           one sundown over and
the heat and red of desert into night

and long ago the young bravura flight
of an artist to celebrate the day
toward its end
           inviting another
to arc above the grass in the unknown

PEAK

late in summer at altitude
and even so a dragonfly
and even so a flower with
a name that did not have one

or a might-have-been combining
the word tiny and the word blue
and now on its unmoving way
into the mountain's shadow

WEATHER WIND

summer had laid the county open and posed
in yellow and golden green and butterscotch
not leaving however at the written time

carrying on a warm wind of new power
that might have taken all the leaves down if they
had been turned enough and made a grove of twig

to howl in but having no tall wheat to mill
or mow the wind did not sound until it reached
the greater cottonwoods where it effected

gesticulations of their every branch
approximating a weather there and might
have seemed to roar even rage to anyone

living at the farm but none was and out in
the open a hawk went on countering it

BUTTE

the ones I would want to meet
in Harding County are set
for tedium now and so
am I
        the heat time over
        the shadow of a windmill
        getting farther north and east
        on the prairie
but I want
to return where the high land
begins and look out west from
the top of a white cliff and
take the pine air
        give tribute
        to all the departing light
        I would not have walked in if
        I had not been
and meet them
who have liked the earth the way
I do
        on top of a butte
        in Harding County
the few
that would be ready to come
a few more in memory

WIDENING THE ZONE

the floodings have driven the city up
and away to heights behind new earthwork
and it may not hem the river again

which has a wider reclamation zone
and paven path and belvedere give in
to different categories of mud

a flight of whitetail deer in overgrowth
marks out the penumbra around them that
will be a part of the water's umbra

geranium plot and croquet field were
intruding on muskrat allodium
and the river has made room for its own

DAUGHTER

in the village of chicken wire
she was three and the faint winter sun
came in the room by a south window
enlarging her mind

the white she could see out there belonged
to what Daddy said and the radio

in her own farmhouse on the prairie
she was thirty and the hard white sun
kept teeming the garden and she watched
from a south window

her mind would forget the radio
but count the day and time Daddy went

VACANT FARMSTEAD IN AUTUMN

there are millennia of sea
                of high grass
in what I have said
and written about one death on
the prairie
          human times were not
awaited that came in eighteen
eighty-six to till and husband
              make a place of
what had been no
more than a part and to kindle
children burying some where the
main grove is now
          nonhuman times
returned for half a century
as though
             but not
    to inhibit
other settlements
             which happened
anyhow and brought grandmother
and granddaughter to plant and ward
and have this earth by heart
         the one
staying on to be the next death
at the farmstead
            I have written
and said about that in twenty
eleven and I am watching
a goldfish move among its dead
      the water is unclean
            the pond
should be emptied of it and of

the fish but there is no one here
to do it and how can I with
millennia in mind
        the farm
reverting to prairie alone
again and fall and in no need
of any sentiment or hand

CHICKEN WIRE

you saw Wyoming's day- and moonless nighttime
when you rode the divide in a backseat and
took home from there a dream of western upland

the prairie town where your family got by
had a chicken-wire fence so you could not
run away but looking through it you almost

made out a distant light-brown poetry in
whatever a cowboy or even a law-
or a badman said and did and you noted

another poetry in the green of both
a holt along the trail and the felt on an
awaiting poker table in Laramie

you grew to when you went in quest on your own
to the country of never a letdown and
you hunted your love up every next draw

returning words to the prairie but you had
to wait for age to tell it was taking home
to write it that made the western dream come out

no need for an ascription of happily
to how you go from low- to upland and back
only of knowingly in the codger way

if you did not have a plot to retreat to
with a chicken-wire fence you would never
get a line of the divide country written

LIVE TO TELL

it may be the interring motion
of rain one day in autumn
        of snow
that would tire you
              may be only
the memories in it moving down
to the braided-wire fence around
a graveyard
        a childhood that might have
been your own on prairie and river
that were
              you saw
       the hanging heavy
chain of another fence within and
wet on the headstone it protected
            light snow
      motioning
the women in
the car not talking and you wanted
to sleep and crows you had not met were
awaiting the interment
            you got
cold to the hucklebones more than one
time too but in autumn you did not
tire
        only waited on a branch
              you stayed up
and now you live to tell

NOVEMBER MORNING

I could not help but see a train
move slow into a cranny on
the wooded horizon
      if it
had whistled I could not have helped
but hear in my fall morning of
no emergency
      dispraising
the engineer and it had not
      the woods
were gray with wild turkey
and the tocking of train on bridge
only marked the silence
      I could
not help but know even if I
was not telacoustic or at
the river
      there had come and would
again a shotgun blat and an
entrailing of gray and red in
the morning
      not today on mine

GO TO THE CAW

I remember a bison meadow
the stuffy day and the gray and heat
my headache but more the yearning talk
of the two whose manikin I was

both regret and yearning in their tone
as if to admit they had been wrong
not coming out earlier to watch
not acting on a dream of bison

they might have had the dream of a dream
been yearning only for a mind to
take in all nature and the grand West
to let them heed the call of their kind

from late middle age I remember
a new young inmate celebrating
when we that ran the prison let him
move in with his fellow sureños

go dream with his kind of the women
and the money awaiting outside
a chance to behead for El Narco
live on in corrido enfermo

I remember hearing on a walk
what seemed to be a crow jamboree
the hard windy sky of November
no mitigating white on the ground

they headed toward it one by one
often two by two or three by three
each adding to the unseen whoopla
in a tree up the river somewhere

larruping the air without regret
with only a yearning to join in
that made the old manikin I was
want to go to the caw of their kind

LINES TO A POTTER

REK

an ash tree sawn and piled on ground
the color of its name and bark
and of its heartwood and somewhere
a clay to be dug up and pugged
that you would turn and manage on
your wheel making a thing to coat
in glaze and fire out of time

a red in the open ash wood
and dead weeds of a dry winter
and bark the gray of what fire
would leave but mug or vase and not
the man that made them surviving
not hand but handiwork taking
all you were and saw out of time

VACANT FARMSTEAD IN WINTER

I have heard the whicker of people
on the sundeck but the wooden chairs
are upended now
               some Haydn from
the potting studio where only
a chill and quiet are remaining
in hampered daylight

       who blew snow out
of the drive will not be around and
the nuthatches will not dominate
at the bird feeder
              no one in the
porch window to see them anyway
or to refill it

       the cat went too
so nestlings will get to fly in May
and the May will be
              field mice teeming
the unmown yard grass overtaking
and then an autumn of pugmarked dirt
of yellow and madder in the grove

MEDLEYS

the river lapsed and turned hard white
and the ground remained a medley
of brown and dun in patches

midwinter had not come to much
but where were the men and women
and children on the dry walks

any meeting under the trees
or bridge would have been a run-in
and they had known it somehow

only the bald eagle wanted
to have one and kept not too high
where open water showed dark

the day became a medley of
quiet and cawing and it would
have been different in snow

A YEAR AND TWO DEATHS

it did not rain or later snow
when they went and could the earth have
been more awake
      its soil time dry
and the flesh time they were in could
not have been more transilient
          yet time
has not an and to it
remaining onefold to be seen
in a river
      felt in a wind
          where they were
until birth into
the animal and are now so
why put a date on moments of
no change and mourn them in writing
      the earth's
awake to rain or snow

MAKING IT BOON

when winter came bad in the meaning
of Milton to the Bay Colony
they looked where children lay under earth
and a weighty firmament and snow
    each had a turn at quoting the Book
    milling it over in mind

such winter would come to a fewer
on the plains of the territory
two centuries away but the Word
and a white-weighted land were the same
    man and woman praying in a hut
    the hidden grave of a child

if winter came dry and not so bad
with grave and garden patches open
nobody would need the counterweight
of Milton or the Book to last it
    only sticks and a match among them
    to make it a boon winter

CONSIDERING

maybe the red-rock country in my mind
has turned to fretwork and I take only
an averted look at the picture of
it there
      the January around me
on the Red River has become too mild
for dormancy in willow or man and
the rocks too far and faint away to draw
me out
      no one on the Colorado
would welcome me and no more than one would
miss me here so whatever I do will
not be a clutch move
      only a saunter

WINTER CHRONICLE

the sun in midwinter reaching forenoon
will move behind the heights of a hotel
and let shadow on my front room and I
accept it and I like to measure the
duration of the eclipse
                    watch it go
from eighteen to thirteen minutes into
a lighter January when I note
the balance in time of sun ebb and flow
and remember that the word tide meant time
to the northmen and means it
        but a change
of health or weather can be violent
with an onset not a sedate decline
to the moment of plague or bone breaking
or tornado and recovery slow
a mind picture of how good the world was
until the event embittering the
valetudinarian
                  or the one
at work in the rubble with claw hammer
and gloves and I have known injury and
wreckage and illness and have gotten old
enough to take both an easy change and
the yank of another
        I live up north
but am not a man of Hoonah getting
much more midwinter sun but even if
I were I would accept the chronic rain
the way I do the time watch in my room
that will be on tomorrow
                    not next month

TAKEN EAST

every train was another again
but the headlight on the engine of none
came as herald and the horn that sounded
in the mind of whoever waited at
the crossing had no taurine or ursine
bellow to it though it meant get away
nor were the cars parading or seeming
to be when they ticked through the prairie town
of hutments and a hoodoo church at three
in winter and the morning
                          was only
another every train again with
one more load of the prairie's unmaking
and whoever waited there saw it go

2010

YOUNG IN THE CITY

whoever she was and whoever you were
had come into town during an agreement
of time and place
                     found everything so right
you needed to meet to maintain the sunlight
on tree and avenue and the perfect sea
     the Arboretum
and the park it was in
were not enough when you wanted the limbs of
the City and looked up itching whenever
a music or a bean-cake odor got strong
               hurried even
to read the admonishment
on a church clock tower OBSERVE THE TIME AND
FLY FROM EVIL to the minute you met in
the Tea Garden with Buddha directing you
to a flower thicket
       whoever she was
whoever you were did not maintain a time
a place or anything and you if not she
read another injunction in the green of
the same Arboretum
                   would fly from people

EXOTERICA

your uncalculated surview
of the beach that time let forenoon
color into memory which
would not need the name Point Reyes

you turned landward with a seal's eye
and would calculate in other
time the way to the wind timber
on the noon of Abineau Peak

you wanted to leave a tooth in
the sand where forenoon had color
and on a mountain of some name
the noon pine were outliving you

AIRPORT IN AUGUST

a cricket on the walk and
a grasshopper in the field
and not another one of
either and a dragonfly
becoming a many and
if I could turn my head more
I would know how many and
few were too but I am not
on a hop or a flight to
Magnolia Avenue
in a town of way out there
though I have a wider range
of emotion and could be

FOR TWO

away to Mendocino and a green tent
for two not made for two
                        no human other
in the campground and a quiet winter sea
          not many
to watch the barman concoct a
gin alexander and only two meeting
the new year in gin moonlight
                    two and a fox
          and the meadow

away from the mania
or mere levity of the bay
                    away to
          Mendocino
          a tent in gray-pine morning
and on again to a city made for two

SKILLMAN LANE

red pantiles on a roof across the lane
and Sonoma Mountain unmoving too
but it was time for night now

a bottle of red wine on the table
and a violin concerto playing
but it was time for talk now

we talked and so became other people
and I drove out in the June night alone
to show how it had to be

and none of the other men and women
we looked up to had known one another
and would not even have met

but she had not wanted any of this
to be or have me be any other
she had wanted only me

I turned myself into other people
to cut away from one that loved me more
than who I was could return

an other drove out into the June night
and left a bottle of wine unfinished
the concerto going on

a peacock in a hutch across the lane
and the unseen mountain unmoving too
but it was time for the road

CITY NIGHTS

she was a daughter of the house
on El Camino del Mar where
I did not exist
                an import
from the Mediterranean
where spice had turned into perfume
and resin into the gems of
a hidden garden
        from Munich
along her way to another
coast of sun and pomegranate
                to be home
at twenty in the
doting house that let her hide me
a night or two in all the need
and confusion of her high room
       where I
did not exist on El
Camino del Mar
                not longer

DAY FALL

FOR SEAJ

it would happen in the afternoon's aging
with sun on the wall and no movement

an abrupt yet intricate modulation
of temperature humidity and light

a resettling down in the air too quick to
catch ahead of its effect on the garden

nicotiana with a richer smell now
and more impendent gold in the one stray cloud

I would have been alone with me and good at
day fall but in vacancy the next minute

the mere wooden bench at the wall not the same
where an other had waited to turn and look

the aging of afternoon would make it my
own again and refix me in solitude

a way to hold onto the rest of my time
and the evening come out not down or yet

ACCORD IN MENDOCINO

wind chiming from a harlequinade
of tent at the meadow's other end

foghorn on out there to note the point
of narrowing visibility

matted winter greens in the park with
an intenser March green dappling them

wet-fern-wood odor and the dying
peep of half a slug in a snake mouth

rain or salt air and a flowering
up again to reach heightened daylight

wind chiming in an overtone of
the very foghorn's fundamental

hand-tuning work without a doubt but
no hand in the wind action or fog

to wonder at the decay or the
perennity of everything

THE PARTS IN YOUR LIFE

LG 1967–2013

you played the baby in rooms that were full
of Jack Teagarden and did not want us
to bundle you away to quieter
and that might have been the affecting turn
of all the many you were made to take

we went on an American highway
but what you got to hear was Manuel
de Falla so you had to be the child
of two that did not mean to destine you
but might have taken an afflicting turn

you played a young girl at the ranch and one
day ran and tripped over the scent patch of
nicotiana in bloom and waited
and that might have been the infecting turn
of all the many of your own you took

QUISCALES DE MÉJICO

I read among the potted mandarinos
on the roof garden and told no one about
the forenoon light

            but the we that were had a
hand in moving a sky of grackle toward
vespertino

            however the tiles of the
roof garden might have been in midday color
I kept to me

            but the we that were had a
name for what they faded to when the grackles
went down and quieted in an unseen park

IF WE WERE

a street named Balboa had to have sea
at the end of it and the foghorn we
awoke to might have been a sea lion

even on the heights that cleared by noon an
odor of marine animality
got to us and later the apartment

we had not met to be up in sunlight
and love out a year nor were we thinking
to talk it over in the briny quilt

we joined every moan of foghorn or
animal when the breeding night came on
that did not need word only deed of us

even now we could take Balboa to
Land's End and look out at redemption in
no other sunlight if there were a we

SONOMA

partying with Theokritos in a library
dirt ice and north wind awaiting out there was not to
be on a hill he might have known yet time did not mean
among madrone at the foot of it and travel's end
and July became panic grass in a dry meadow
where a few oak and juniper he might have walked to
did not move in thymish air nor would the heat and a
midday made for goat rut turned gentler when the
etesian came up
          he would have known however
what the added gentling of wine had done and that each
catclaw and rattler fang had a match in the moment
country's mind and doubted the urgent red flowering
on a white garden wall for a cut that happened in
the next bay-tree or rock shadow
          maybe the Miwok
had looked to the edges of beauty and the hidden
infliction too and though only mind had taken him
to Sonoma the Greek might have known it so would not
have had to repeat that no one can be one with sun
whether in a vineyard or a printed memory

EDUCATION

did I have to go through city
to make it here
                have to listen
to jackhammers on a morning
that had been white-wine otherwise

to mate in the arboretum
during lime spring
                walk a goat path
over the beauty hill and home
where dog and man were feculent

have to get drunk and almost ram
a woman's Jag
                reach the summit
of Mount Diablo tomorrow
on a New Year's hangover hike

maybe if I had not been in
any redwoods
                done mimicry
shooting pool with the violent
at midnight I would not have made

it here so maybe it had not
been a delay
                a distraction
after all and maybe city
got me to mean and keep the word

THE WINE OF IT

who not born to madrone or
poppy fields of orange would have
wanted chard in the garden and
a shrubby footpath to the hill

I married madrone and bay
and the smell of pittosporum
and owned nicotiana too
and bell peppers in the garden

who left had only the right to
remember but I keep the wine
of it all with me and can see
my adobe wall over there

IT SEEMED

THE MOON STAYED FULL LAST MONTH
              —FERLINGHETTI

to one that could not
turn from the window
or opening
            to
whom month and moment
would be one at the
last and at last
            my
full moon will remain
invariably
the night I do not

from "Big Sur Light" by Lawrence Ferlinghetti
in *How to Paint Sunlight*, New York, 2001

TRUTH IN SAN FRANCISCO

I knew that I was foreign
    not who
in a town of talkative gargoyles
but ungothic light where no one had
to wait to meet Punchinello e
Giuditta on the stage of park or
avenue nor Ferlinghetti and
Duncan
        Brautigan
    each a walking
overstatement with cap and bells to
the eye of an other

        in the name
of what I saw the troupers that way
who knew but reading them did not make
me want to get onto the platform
    only to stay
a foreigner and
not fake a twitch of aporia
in lingo not my own at an all-
night graisserie

        the town offered me
a ticket to midway make-belief
but it was not round-trip so I took
the next boat to the Farallones

OREGONIAN TEXT

how to translate a ditch of bramble prick
with hidden moving water or mad green
blearing in window and windshield or the
runny sky not open every day
to show a gray denuded mountainside
way up and out
                rhinovirus winter
in wet but the chill not enough to crimp
any smoke of fir brush or mill wigwam
and at night even a wood-cinder glint
on the highway then yew or hemlock air
and the subjugating of faint dawn by
another cloud
                how to translate it all

NO RETURN

IT IS EASIER TO DIE THAN TO REMEMBER
—Basil Bunting

when she turned to me under the madrone
the April did not have to do with her

the morning flank of Sonoma Mountain
did rather with sun and bay and live oak

why had I taken a blonde of night to
walk in a clearing that would expose her

and not noticed anyway wanting to
give her and me the moment in a name

one I had known as springtime waited on
the other flank but I did not go back

ARISE

when you woke young in the tent and morning
and spring with a memory of the wine
and love that had made your night you could see
all the redwood arriving and wanted
to join the whiskey jack on a picnic

when you woke old and alone in the tent
and morning and spring with no memory
of love or wine or the night you could see
the lake sky widen and wanted to join
the crow or were there two on a picnic

2008

CAMP ON THE LITTLE MISSOURI

the lands were not bad in a way
one late and not-gone summer with
orange high clinker-rock and dwarf
juniper and a turned leaf or
two in the air to see from the
tenting ground that heat had basined

a whim of wind seemed overdue
to bring up the cool river air
in the dun of evening or
clouding and at the idea
of weather front a matted horse
that had known no rider walked by

not whim but spreeing of wind in
the night and a few rain pellets
hit at the tent but did not wet
or topple a thing and the dark
went on too long to permit a
remake of cicada forenoon

what it was raining about who
knew the day that came with more than
a word of chill or whether to
do a man's rain imitation
and weep over the muddy lands
which were bad in no other way

JULY IN WYOMING

admit to being frayed and too late for
money- or woman-making ambition

let the prairie be acedia and
take another road out of it to a

red-chalk river bank and quakenasp that
mark one point on the way to the mountain

rabbit up there may not know hiking man
enough to run and young bull snake rather

wait in morning sun-warm trail than hide so
give no hawk-wing flap to either but

turn a sleepy eye toward the ridge and
do not claim any pine or rockfall there

telling what happens now would write it in
legend and make imaginary time

mountain is where to be and who and what-
ever next too late for reprehension

REST STOP

Big Horn County

the monument was only a hitch
in the heat of your long drive north and
you wanted a roadside park but went
east on a not-much-taken highway
feeling the day's wear but thinking of
the cavalry
    your drive or ride was
hard yet it would have been harder to
be driven or ridden toward the
ridge and coulee and the sweat of that
final hurt and now you were coming
to a green patch
    some lawn behind a
cottonwood row it seemed would let you
have the walk and drink you had not quite
earned but you did not see where to turn
in until you reached the gate of the
cemetery
    the cowboys and these
whoever here had died like the men of
the cavalry and were not dead in that they
were not any more than you would be
after death put only another
hitch in the heat of your ride or drive

EAST OF WALLA WALLA

one time ago a three went riding
into the Palouse
          late afternoon
and I was the boy of them to end
July with an arm out the window

the too-warm air had a berry smell
or other on it
          orchard maybe
and my eye did not want the shadows
to get any longer in the ditch

no time ago a one came riding
into the Palouse
          late afternoon
but I had a nose of the world now
and knew witch hazel when I smelled it

SUMMER RANGE

the way led out to an overlook
on caprock and not far to the north
some high cumulonimbi went gold
      too late
in the day for rain I thought
and did not hear an omen but there
was movement among them
      at one edge
another among the bison in
the canyon ahead
      an action or
reaction that had a few quitting
the graze and turning to see no more
than I did nor was a threat at work
on the clouds' bright edge
      they were only
concerting with a change of wind or
other
      the bison were concerting
        concenting
with it too whatever
it happened to be and finally
I got it
      but with only the mind
of a potshooter how could I say

DRIFTER'S TUNE

if I went out of the prefecture of snow
to the red-rock country I would love again

and if I did would I climb high in the day
or get back there for an emptiness only

I am not the same one that went riding out
to Mesa County in a different time

and the trails that I knew would be other too
with a new who and when and where at the end

I want to go up high on Indian Point
to find a not just any someone waiting

if I went out of the prefecture of snow
I would take both love and emptiness again

BADLANDS OF A METACOWBOY

                bangtail herd
in the road to Wind Canyon
were slow to let my big skunk wagon through
and one foal's eye reminded me of the
look a too-young indita had given
on the sundown way in Tamaulipas
        I had been
a younker then so she might
have put a dream in it but now the foal
with a mossy-horn wrangler in view got
the same brown eye or look of reckoning
not only human and animal too
              even more
I would want to reponder
as I rode to meet an only and stub-
horn buffalo bull at the canyon gate
who was having him another day and
hardly needed to look to tell I was
        no pilgrim
with camera and I knew
to sit and not begrudge him the waitout
that I was the foal the indita and
the bull and might have been a hadrosaur
having me another day
            old Duckbill

BELONG

when there is nothing home to keep you
the road out of prairie to mountain
will open
        take your everyday
to the desert canyon of its map
and it will not be on the coal train
heading east
              magpie and vulture you
have met will meet you again in a
rose-rock country you have wanted but
never seen
        more than a memory
of juniper scent will draw you up
a trail and make you content to live
the morning
           to think with every
dead skunk or woodchuck on the road out
of mountain to prairie how much you
belong to
        you can go home again
when nothing is in it
to keep you

METACOWBOY LETS ON TO CATTLE KATE

I did not have the word to tell me what you were
and I mistook the cupid's cramp for ache of age

the day we met you got to fussing over me
and I the same to you and how were we to know

there is a word for what you left me in the rain
another day at the cantina when we talked

but if I wrote it out the two of us would laugh
so I am belly through the brush up Kannah Creek

CHANSON DE GESTE OF A METACOWBOY

> and hear one bird
> sing terribly afar in the lost lands
> —CUMMINGS

I saw her through the eye of another
and camera where she happened to be
on an overlook crag at noon sometime

the Green or the Bighorn in quick June shine
ahead down there and I did not know which
with young slim Kate not facing the other

giving her every attention to
the part of Wyoming that she had found
and I had lost for all I remember

I reckoned it had been to catch the sight
of that yellow hair and no further why
I rode so many coulees in my day

and made so many a crag height into
a lookout tower else no man I knew
would have hit any trail whatsoever

I had to seek the Kate of the photo
even if I did not get to find her
or whoever had held the camera

SCION OF A COPPERHEAD

it might have been the heartache word
of eighteen sixty-five that sent
my bunch riding upwind to where
no other hurt would overtake

I am my great-great-granddaddy
and the range is Wyoming now
and I head on much as he did
for the same haven of sunset

if you are wanting to track me
look there but I think you should know
you will not see a picket sign
or any way to my wagon

I water in fear at nighttime
and you will have to wait to find
me with a bib and a drool in
a home not far outside Gillette

CHANTS FROM "NO ONE OTHER"

they needed not call you Ishmael
unblest unburdened with fame or money
no one on way with no one other
you slipped the country drunk at night
and you can see it ever now
this very movement

they needed not call you Henry David
who had not built a chicken coop in
San Francisco Flagstaff Fargo
if I went eighty-five would die
you thought but did so anyway
y no volveráááás

they needed not call you John Crowe Ransom
the many ties you had not been wearing
psych-tech poet in old Crown Vic
you slipped the country drunk at night
a trail had ever been for you
some red arroyo

they needed not call you Jedediah
her pretty mouth so full of chew
y no volveráááás
you heard it Texmex radio
another leg the same great trek
midnight vibrato

they needed not call you Lazarus
unblest unburdened with some one other
to want you to stay or return
you might retire to Boca Linda

they needed not call you Cyrano
lover on road with loved one other
the moment seemed to be for two
at Bodega Head or Mazatlán
or Mendocino the both of you there
ocean long away

they needed not call you Everyman
who only anywhere just arrived
no one on way with no one other
you might have been a chaparral cock
and you can see it ever now
this very movement

they needed not call you Edward Abbey
the wend of the road was maritime
you fucked a mermaid in the water
and slipped the country drunk at night
running to mountain desert plain
y no volveráááás

they needed not call you San Francesco
a bird is meant to be watched oh my
eat of the tree like no one other
you slipped the garden drunk at night
and on thy belly shalt thou go
in la povertààààà

they needed not call you Wendell Berry
to cover the ground is to love it
there will never be another
like your everlovin mother
if you went eighty-five would die
did so anyway

they needed not call you Fridjof Nansen
neither a Japanese man nor a cat
no one on way with no one other
you slipped the winter right at dawn
and you could see it ever now
on Indian Point

OUT

I am not seen in rodeo
      shitkicker
   or
      Stetson
  but
on Friday I turned into an
openly cowboy poet

I would not have to strum on the
      clairseach
  smoke a
     dudeen
  wear
green or smell of the bog to be
an Irish poet would I

would only have to write in Erse
Microsoft Word has the font
though it might do to know the pith
of Ireland's dreaming too

I have got the American
western heart by heart
   half of
the dialect that it used to
live and is living on in

give me no
      batwings

any day
no high
          war bonnet
neither
all I need to make a hand is
the lingo of hootowl swag

      clairseach   Irish harp
      dudeen   Irish clay pipe

NOTE TO MIAMI BEACH

I did not win my spurs on Collins Avenue
and now may be a cowboy l=a=n=g=u=a=g=e poet
trying to hoot along with missa cantata
at a fire you have made of palo verde
when all you would want me to do is nonrefer
                oh I
am just a rhinestone saddle bum like you
lopin high from one performance gig to the next
but even with many lingos in the conk case
I aint quite no Cimmerian book boyero
de Cimarrón
                    let my range word on that be sung

YELLOW SPRINGS

they saw me but did not know who I was
or knew who I was but did not see me

they let me be until it was too late
so that they had to laisser faire for good

I lived on what I did not have to do
and had no reason to go on running

in flight or was it pursuit but it took
me to Oregon Guanajuato Mu-

nich the edge of Toroweap overlook
not that anything cracked my solitude

the more I moved the whollier it got
which contradicted the notion of who

had seen me and not known that I would need
one place to squat if I wanted alone

I do not aim to slow my moving on
unless I get to Yellow Springs tonight

POET GUY IN AMERICA

he had gotten a talking job that tied him to
rooms so tried to act it out in them
        play the trek
        driver the
        screamy bitch
        the wiiiild turkey
                dreaming
that somewhere a camera waited whereon he
would be limelit to the pattycake music of
pander man and win all fame and money and sex
        while
he might have ridden on the untalkative
plains to write it out
        a soothfast metacowboy

OUT OF SEDONA

you did take note of my long o in the word ON
the hint of a drawl that matched my pearly buttons
and might have led another to divine a half
continent of nineteenth-century opini-
onation behind them
              not you
                  the weather-worn
sunny grin did not distract you from my lack of
bolo tie or my hand's unhardened feel under
the tan or what my lowboy red sedan implied
you did take one more margarita even though
you had never met a metacowboy had you

METACOWBOY

erst came I boots in saddle
to them melanotic hills

now I am ridin buckboard
to get the deadwood on him

      SO HUA

erst came I with the wind and
dropped me into night in song

now this here metacowboy
will zing him to Rankin Ridge

      SO HUA

CANYON

I rode with all of my worldly wisdom to Toroweap
          my political savvy
reached the overlook
at sundown out toward the middle of May
          it must have
been nine so I had time to do the tent
          sit on
a rock and watch as well it must have taken my eye and
mind a minute to touch the desert river
          the
canyon already shading into a grey blue down there
Lava Falls a dim silent movie of itself
          what could any
man have said or written to such a depth
          I did not even get a satori
          no man
needed to there
          I just rode out with a notion of self
intact at sunup have been on that kind of drift
until today
          now I know I have no worldly wisdom
          no political savvy
not how or why just
that I have yet to find a limit to the dark depth of
your eyes
          could go on forever and on in it

OLD SONG

I used to be the one leaving them sedentary
when I headed ever and often out to the West
a sunshine rider whom their lorn thinking prodded on
I used to be leaving them sedate

this time you have made the trail to Wyoming your own
I am the one abandoned to condominiums
I miss you with a lump in the rawhide whole of me
that won't be going down tomorrow

ANY HOUR

I was on the move in the black of morning
to get the tea water ready and live
        had known
it in San Diego the march to
chow
        out of
Santa Rosa the hallu-
cinatory drive home in it from a night
job
        the hour had been mine ever since

too many endings of love have toughened what
should not have been
        I had felt too quick to
seal over and
        ride on
                would almost prefer
                to want to die
this resignation too
handy I had thought
                an old buck nun don't know
                the lonesome until a cupid cramp lay
                hold on him
        yet in
the unlight morning of his mind
        hootowl hollow will be waiting

the clouds had not raveled away by mid-
autumn afternoon
        it would not get warm
and I headed out walking no matter on

a path I had yet to try along the
Sheyenne
                        one more cold
                        yinland season
                I had
                thought
                        and I am off
which brought a kind of
yangland warmth already but more was to it
than that
                the wondrous mere mundanity
of sagehen love had pooled around me on the
way who had been its wanted aim and end
                I could
remember
                she might have been saying
the name of me then and again when I
returned to my hollow
                the rooms like the
ragged empty park were holy
with her now
                I could stay or ride anytime

EVEN THE WORD

it seemed I was pelado at that outfit
the top screw came to where I wrangatanged
and told me hasta la vista
            big augur
did not have to
            so I heard the owl hoot
another time am riding the coulees on
my own again oh
                  the critter within
                  he ain't got no chin
          I have but only one
regret to leave that sagehen of the heart
who freighted my crop with more than muckamuck
            we mean to write
but how will she reach me
in care of sundown
            will take a longer while
than I have to get serene
        to let
                you
into any other song even the word

NOTA BENE

even the time you were gone went quick
even the hurt in your place in me
did not make the days any longer

maybe to you on the trail they were
when it led you from time to mountain
maybe I'm out of your memory

FROM SCRATCH

I am from scratch and go toward death
whithersoever I ride
        hame-head
        Swede
        knothead cowboy
                går mot döden

I may be out on the Black Hills now
have not wound up however
        in a
        whittle
        rock with Sir
        Isaac Nutant

point me the trail to
                det ryggbrutna
                berget
I would not wink
        anywise
        one more
        cowbunny
        might turn me though

keep me a minute from the riding
                mot döden
that I am on
        north of
        Laramie

to some
own bone orchard

går mot döden   go toward death
det ryggbrutna berget   the broken-back mountain

BREAK OF MARCH

easy winter went into obduration
at the break of March
        I turned my scope
toward the foothills then where the color would
start but
                no
           she said
who did not know
much of the mountain
                keep it on the summit
                ridge that's
                where vernality will show
who did not own
a word like that
                but I had
to heed the smile on her and what I
could see
                a fuller white
                chromatic
                not of snow
took my mind up there to bathe
in the ions already
                she came along

YUMA HAT

when I lived in smoke heat on the Clearwater of
Idaho I knew that the river would exhale
into my late-evening rooms if I opened them
but now I am in the dog days on the Red of
North Dakota and the water will be hot as
afternoon all night
        why do I walk out along
the bike and inline-skating path when I could have
oak shade
        I am thinking about
        American
        poetry
of
                Harold Bloom
                Garrison Keillor
a pharisee and a puritan antholo-
gizing it into the human future of a
world that does not have one
        not about my grandchild
or
                Hawaii
        cannot stand to do that
        I turn
around where men have made a heap of boulders that
have no right home in the drought-cracked mud flats here and
amid them an only sunflower is working
toward tall and I hear the clamant young voice of
a crow on the woody other bank
        why do I
get hello a smile
        every young brown woman
        of them I meet
not one afoot however

>   they
>   go wheeling
> away from the last elm in the world
>   maybe
> they know that I have nothing on under
> my skin or maybe it is my old Yuma hat

ANY OTHER

unknowing young would let a dream of other
take them to the high south country or they might
wait into the wealth of unforgetting age
and I am a mind to go to Cuenca too
be white-haired Rhodo among the Quechua
meet Rosía in a mountain hut
           but why
should I want more company when I only
tolerate my own and even with a warm
smoked woman next to me would be of larger
mind to trek alone way in the nonhuman
Andes
              write it but not in Incan or the
Cuenca lingo
              neither would get me out of
me and Rosía not either who'd glut me
on a same
              nothing human is an other
while undreamt mountain and prairie and canyon
and shore are any of what I want to see

JOHN WAHL

(1950–2003)

you were a lone trekker like me
so we did not ever get to
open that half pint of cognac
at the same campfire and late
sundown
          you went hard on man and
yourself that time you humped into
an unwarranted May snowfall
in the Toiyabe and even
more so at the end
          but you did
know where the poems were
and when

METACOWBOY AT APRIL'S END

big snow the other day not wet enough
and too much a spark in the night-room air
and time between hay and grass will not quit
so why hang and rattle
        I am a mind
to fog out to the uraninite range
where sage grouse are dwindlin too but a free
ranger can go unshucked in light and hot
on the Little Mo
        do not have to find
a lek of my own to make chin music
in with buck-nun days accretin though I
have an eye and if a sagehen come on
I would not die in my tree
        or sagebrush

POWDER RIVER

would be hard in dancing boots to maintain
the stride of a militant and I am
known to ride but I do not have to get
there quick anymore
                take to the coulees
either avoiding some young maenad or
the lap of uxory in froward flight
            I
do not have to reach that beckoning
mountain at all and not a callico
in Cheyenne would mind that much if I went
fogging out
                what I have now is home range
and time and evening sun to study
monadology in and am content
enough but I have got the war bag packed

Biography

Drawing by Trygve Olson

Born in North Dakota, Rodney Nelson came of age during the nineteen sixties, the end of which found him in San Francisco with an editing job at China Books & Periodicals. He witnessed many of the social events of that turbulent era but opted not to be an active part of them. He was drawn to solitude in nature. Later, he worked as a licensed psychiatric technician and a copy editor, the latter in Arizona, where he also evolved into a backcountry trekker. When time cued him, he chose to return to his birthplace "for the endgame," as he put it. This seemed to prompt an unexpected "late flowering" in poetry. Some of his book and chapbook titles are *Mogollon Picnic, Hill of Better Sleep, Felton Prairie, In Wait, Cross Point Road, Late & Later, The Western Wide, Billy Boy, Ahead of Evening, Winter in Fargo, Hjemkomst, Canyon, Time Tacit,* and *Minded Places.*

www.ingramcontent.com/pod-product-compliance
Lightning Source LLC
Chambersburg PA
CBHW051835090426
42736CB00011B/1824